IT'S
NOT
ABOUT ME
ME
Journal

IT'S NOT ABOUT ME

Journal

MAX LUCADO

INTEGRITY®
PUBLISHERS
Nashville

It's Not About Me Journal

Published by Integrity Publishers, a division of Integrity Media, Inc., 5250 Virginia Way, Suite 110, Brentwood, TN 37027.

HELPING PEOPLE WORLDWIDE EXPERIENCE *the* MANIFEST PRESENCE *of* GOD.

Cover/Interior design by UDG / Designworks, Sisters, Oregon.

Produced with the assistance of The Livingstone Corporation (www.LivingstoneCorp.com). Project staff includes Dave Veerman, Ashley Taylor, and Mary Horner Collins.

ISBN 1-59145-205-8

Printed in the United States of America
04 05 06 07 08 LBM 9 8 7 6 5 4 3 2 1

INTRODUCTION

This companion journal to Max Lucado's book *It's Not About Me* has been designed to help you grab hold of a God-centered life—and along with it, all the deep satisfaction and fulfillment that such a life alone offers. You can use the quotes, questions, and Bible verses in this thirty-day journal to help you mull over the life-changing perspectives of *It's Not About Me* and help them take root in your own life.

Here are a few tips that have helped others to maximize their journaling experience, which you may find helpful:

As you prepare to write, get alone in a quiet, favorite spot. Some people like to play soft background music as they gather their thoughts.

Note the date of your journaling experience.

Read the related chapter from the book before you begin writing, or you may prefer to jot down your thoughts as you read, musing on fresh ideas you encounter.

Be on the lookout for phrases, quotes, and Bible verses that especially grab your attention. Write them down and note your reaction to them.

Following the Bible verses, there is space to write out a prayer to God—expressing thanks, words of praise, or any questions you have.

Explore your feelings as well as your thoughts. Make this an adventure of self-discovery.

Don't be afraid to make lists or sketch out simple drawings.

Begin and end your journaling time with prayer, asking God to lead you into a life that brings him glory and truly satisfies.

When we make the awesome discovery that a God-centered life opens the door to astonishing possibilities, we begin to enjoy what we have longed for all our lives. "Life makes sense when we accept our place," writes Max. "The gift of pleasures, the purpose of problems—all for him. The God-centered life works. And it rescues us from a life that doesn't."

What aspects, if any, in your life are just "not working" right now?

_____

_____

_____

_____

_____

_____

_____

_____

_____

DAY 2
BUMPING LIFE OFF SELF-CENTER

Reflect

"PERHAPS OUR PLACE IS NOT AT THE CENTER OF THE UNI-
VERSE. GOD DOES NOT EXIST TO MAKE A BIG DEAL OUT OF
US. WE EXIST TO MAKE A BIG DEAL OUT OF HIM. IT'S NOT
ABOUT YOU. . . . IT'S ALL ABOUT HIM."

Looking at life from God's perspective can be a radical experience.
His all-importance bumps us off self-center and self-importance. In
any other person this claim would be the height of self-centeredness.
Why is it not self-centeredness in God?

_____

_____

_____

_____

_____

_____

Respond

When people look at your life, they see *something*. How do your choices and values reflect that it's not all about you, but that God is all-important in your life?

_____

_____

_____

_____

_____

_____

_____

_____

_____

_____

_____

_____

_____

Pray and Praise

*"For by him all things were created:
things in heaven and on earth, visible and
invisible, whether thrones or powers or rulers
or authorities; all things were created by him
and for him. He is before all things, and in
him all things hold together."*

(C O L O S S I A N S   1 : 1 6 – 1 7)

_____

_____

_____

_____

_____

_____

_____

_____

_____

_____

ACCEPTING YOUR PLACE
IN THE WORLD

Reflect

"CAN YOU IMAGINE AN ORCHESTRA WITH AN 'IT'S ALL
ABOUT ME' OUTLOOK? EACH ARTIST CLAMORING FOR SELF-
EXPRESSION. . . . CONDUCTOR IGNORED. . . . HARMONY?
HARDLY. . . . WHAT WOULD HAPPEN IF WE TOOK OUR
PLACES AND PLAYED OUR PARTS? IF WE MADE [GOD'S]
SONG OUR HIGHEST PRIORITY? . . . WE MOVE FROM
ME-FOCUS TO GOD-FOCUS BY PONDERING HIM.
WITNESSING HIM. BEHOLDING HIM CHANGES US."

Understanding that life is not all about you adds depth and richness
and purpose to life. Looking to God, you will find what your "place"
is in this world. What does it mean to "behold" Christ and ponder
him?

_____

_____

_____

_____

_____

_____

_____

Respond

As you move toward a God-centered life, what "part" do you think you might have to play? How does focusing on him change your desires and goals?

_____

_____

_____

_____

_____

_____

_____

_____

_____

Pray and Praise

*"Beholding as in a glass the glory of the Lord,
[we] are changed into the same image from glory
to glory, even as by the Spirit of the Lord."*

(2 CORINTHIANS 3:18 KJV)

_____

_____

_____

_____

_____

_____

_____

_____

_____

_____

_____

_____

DAY 4
SHOW ME YOUR GLORY

Reflect

"'SHOW ME YOUR GLORY,' MOSES BEGS. FORGET A BANK;
HE WANTS TO SEE FORT KNOX. . . . YOU AND I NEED WHAT
MOSES NEEDED—A GLIMPSE OF GOD'S GLORY. SUCH A
SIGHTING CAN CHANGE YOU FOREVER."

What does it mean to "see" God's glory? How might it change your
perspective on things?

_____

_____

_____

_____

_____

_____

_____

Respond

What do the things you pray for reveal about you? About your view
of God?

_____

_____

_____

_____

_____

_____

_____

_____

_____

_____

_____

_____

_____

Pray and Praise

"For great is the LORD and most worthy of praise;
he is to be feared above all gods. For all the gods
of the nations are idols, but the LORD made the
heavens. Splendor and majesty are before him;
strength and glory are in his sanctuary. . . .
Ascribe to the LORD the glory due his name; bring
an offering and come into his courts. Worship the
LORD in the splendor of his holiness; tremble
before him, all the earth."

(P S A L M   9 6 : 4 – 6 ,   8 – 9)

_____

_____

_____

_____

_____

_____

_____

_____

DAY 5
CLARIFYING YOUR
GREATEST DESIRE

Reflect

"WHEN OUR DEEPEST DESIRE IS NOT THE THINGS OF GOD
OR A FAVOR FROM GOD, BUT GOD HIMSELF, WE CROSS A
THRESHOLD. LESS SELF-FOCUS, MORE GOD-FOCUS. LESS
ABOUT ME, MORE ABOUT HIM."

In the rush of life, it's often difficult to live with clear goals and
desires. How do you know if you are truly desiring what God has for
you? How do you distinguish between the things you get from God
and God himself?

_____

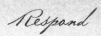
Respond

What are some steps you can take to resist focusing on the gifts and become hungrier for the Giver himself?

_____

_____

_____

_____

_____

_____

_____

_____

_____

_____

_____

_____

_____

Pray and Praise

"I consider everything a loss compared to the surpassing greatness of knowing Christ Jesus my Lord, for whose sake I have lost all things. I consider them rubbish, that I may gain Christ and be found in him."

(P H I L I P P I A N S   3 : 8 — 9)

_____

_____

_____

_____

_____

_____

_____

_____

_____

_____

DAY 6
DIVINE SELF-PROMOTION

Reflect

"God's staff meetings, if he had them, would revolve around one question: 'How can we reveal my glory today?' God's to-do list consists of one item: 'Reveal my glory.' Heaven's framed and mounted purpose statement . . . reads: 'Declare God's glory.' God exists to showcase God."

How do you respond to the Bible's tremendous emphasis on the glory of God? How is God's seeming self-promotion different from human self-promotion?

_____

_____

_____

_____

_____

_____

Respond

God's ways are so much higher than ours. How can you begin to appreciate and enjoy God's glory—his wonder and majesty—in your daily life?

_____

_____

_____

_____

_____

_____

_____

_____

_____

_____

_____

_____

Pray and Praise

"Who has measured the waters in the hollow of his hand, or with the breadth of his hand marked off the heavens? Who has held the dust of the earth in a basket, or weighed the mountains on the scales and the hills in a balance? Who has understood the mind of the LORD, or instructed him as his counselor? Whom did the LORD consult to enlighten him, and who taught him the right way? Who was it that taught him knowledge or showed him the path of understanding?"

(ISAIAH 40:12–14)

_____

_____

_____

_____

_____

_____

_____

_____

FINDING YOUR PURPOSE IN LIFE

Reflect

"GOD AWOKE YOU AND ME THIS MORNING FOR ONE
PURPOSE: 'DECLARE HIS GLORY AMONG THE NATIONS, HIS
MARVELOUS DEEDS AMONG ALL PEOPLES' (1 CHRONICLES
16:24). . . . WHY DO YOU HAVE TALENTS AND ABILITIES?
FOR HIM. EVERYTHING AND EVERYONE EXISTS TO
REVEAL HIS GLORY. INCLUDING YOU."

We often think of a life purpose as something complicated and unknowable at times. But ultimately, everything exists to reveal God's glory. What actions and attitudes are evident in fleshing out this purpose as stated in 1 Chronicles 16:24?

_____

_____

_____

_____

_____

_____

_____

_____

_____

Respond

What other purposes, events, or ideas do you spend most of your
time and energy promoting? What are some practical ways you can
purposefully "declare God's glory"?

_____

_____

_____

_____

_____

_____

_____

_____

_____

_____

Pray and Praise

"There is only one God, the Father, who created everything, and we exist for him."

(1 CORINTHIANS 8:6 NLT)

_____

_____

_____

_____

_____

_____

_____

_____

_____

_____

_____

_____

HOLY DIFFERENT

Reflect

"The Hebrew word for *holy* is *qadosh*, which means cut off or separate. Holiness, then, speaks of the 'otherness' of God. His total uniqueness. Everything about God is different from the world he has made. . . . On the one occasion seraphim appear in Scripture, they endlessly trilogize the same word. 'Holy, holy, holy.'. . . Repetition, in Hebrew, performs the work of our highlighter. It is a tool of emphasis. The six-winged angels do not proclaim him merely holy, . . . he *is* holy, holy, holy."

Holiness is a rather abstract concept. How would you explain it in more concrete terms? What does it mean to *be* holy versus *acting* holy?

_____

_____

_____

_____

_____

_____

_____

_____

Respond

What is your view of God and what he is like? How does this view affect how you live?

_____

_____

_____

_____

_____

_____

_____

_____

_____

_____

_____

_____

Pray and Praise

"Great and marvelous are your deeds, Lord God Almighty. Just and true are your ways, King of the ages. Who will not fear you, O Lord, and bring glory to your name? For you alone are holy. All nations will come and worship before you, for your righteous acts have been revealed."

(REVELATION 15:3-4)

_____

_____

_____

_____

_____

_____

_____

_____

_____

_____

DISCOVERING YOUR HIDDEN STRENGTH

Reflect

"ONE GLIMPSE OF GOD'S HOLINESS, AND ISAIAH CLAIMS
CITIZENSHIP AMONG THE INFECTED AND THE DISEASED. . . .
GOD'S HOLINESS SILENCES HUMAN BOASTING. AND GOD'S
MERCY MAKES US HOLY. . . . GOD, WHO IS QUICK TO
PARDON AND FULL OF MERCY, PURGES ISAIAH OF HIS
SIN AND REDIRECTS HIS LIFE (ISAIAH 6)."

As we come to understand and fear God's holiness, we see more of
who we really are. Why does God's holiness silence human boasting?
Why is our only real strength in him?

_____

_____

_____

_____

_____

_____

Respond

How has God's forgiveness and mercy redirected your own life? In what new ways can you boast about his strength in your life?

_____

_____

_____

_____

_____

_____

_____

_____

_____

_____

_____

_____

_____

_____

Pray and Praise

"May I never boast except in the cross of our Lord Jesus Christ, through which the world has been crucified to me, and I to the world."

(GALATIANS 6:14)

_____

_____

_____

_____

_____

_____

_____

_____

_____

_____

_____

JUST A MOMENT

Reflect

"Everyone has a certain number of moments.
Everyone, that is, except God. . . . Tucked away in
each of us is a hunch that we were made for
forever and a hope that the hunch is true. . . .
If life is 'just a moment' (2 Corinthians 4:17),
can't we endure any challenge for a moment?"

Reflect on the meaning of eternity and the timelessness of God.
What does it mean to you that God is eternal, without beginning or
end? Why is it important to recognize that your life is just a moment
in time, and that you were made for eternity?

_____

_____

_____

_____

_____

_____

_____

_____

_____

Respond

When in your life has heaven seemed most real and this world had its
loosest grip on you?

_____

_____

_____

_____

_____

_____

_____

_____

_____

_____

_____

_____

Pray and Praise

"He has put eternity in their hearts."

(E C C L E S I A S T E S   3 : 1 1   N K J V)

_____

_____

_____

_____

_____

_____

_____

_____

_____

_____

_____

_____

_____

LIVING YOUR LIFE IN THE LIGHT OF ETERNITY

Reflect

"THE HEAVY BECOMES LIGHT WHEN WEIGHED AGAINST
ETERNITY. . . . 'ALL ABOUT ME' COUNSEL SAYS, 'LIFE IS
SHORT—GET OUT.' GOD'S WISDOM SAYS, 'LIFE IS SHORT—
STAY IN.' THE BREVITY OF LIFE GRANTS POWER TO ABIDE,
NOT AN EXCUSE TO BAIL. FLEETING DAYS DON'T JUSTIFY
FLEEING PROBLEMS. FLEETING DAYS STRENGTHEN
US TO ENDURE PROBLEMS."

What does it mean to you to live in the light of eternity? How can a conscious awareness of eternity better equip you for living here and now?

_____

_____

_____

_____

_____

_____

_____

_____

Respond

In what ways has maintaining an eternal perspective made a difference in how you've responded to the momentary trials of life—whether petty irritations or serious difficulties? Why?

_____

_____

_____

_____

_____

_____

_____

_____

_____

_____

Pray and Praise

"Our light affliction, which is but for a moment, is working for us a far more exceeding and eternal weight of glory."

(2 CORINTHIANS 4:17 NKJV)

_____

_____

_____

_____

_____

_____

_____

_____

_____

_____

_____

_____

HIS UNCHANGING HAND

Reflect

"SET YOUR BEARINGS ON THE ONE AND ONLY
NORTH STAR IN THE UNIVERSE—GOD. FOR THOUGH
LIFE CHANGES, HE NEVER DOES. SCRIPTURE MAKES
EYE-POPPING CLAIMS ABOUT HIS PERMANENCE. . . .
'THE SCRIPTURE CANNOT BE BROKEN' (JOHN 10:35,
NKJV). AND SINCE IT CAN'T, SINCE HIS TRUTH WILL
NOT WAVER, GOD'S WAYS WILL NEVER ALTER."

In an always-changing world of uncertainty, what difference does
it make to believe in God's never-changing character? Why is it
important?

_____

_____

_____

Respond

Think about the changes or unexpected events in your life right now.
In what ways does God's permanence and unchanging nature comfort and encourage you?

_____

_____

_____

_____

_____

_____

_____

_____

_____

Pray and Praise

"But the plans of the LORD stand firm forever, the purposes of his heart through all generations."

(PSALM 33:11)

_____

_____

_____

_____

_____

_____

_____

_____

_____

_____

_____

CONQUERING YOUR STRESSES AND UNCERTAINTIES

"WITH CHANGE COMES FEAR, INSECURITY, SORROW,
STRESS. . . . GOD'S PLANS WILL NEVER CHANGE, BECAUSE
HE MAKES HIS PLANS IN COMPLETE KNOWLEDGE. . . .
NOTHING TAKES HIM BY SURPRISE."

God is all-knowing and sovereign. Are you convinced that our God is
in control and worthy of absolute trust? Why or why not?

_____

_____

_____

_____

_____

_____

_____

_____

_____

_____

Respond

How does God's unchanging nature reassure you right now in the midst of the uncertainties and stresses of life? In what ways have you seen his plans worked out in your own life?

_____

_____

_____

_____

_____

_____

_____

_____

_____

_____

"*The* LORD *is exalted, for He dwells on high; . . .
Wisdom and knowledge will be the
stability of your times.*"

(I S A I A H   3 3 : 5 — 6   N K J V)

_____

_____

_____

_____

_____

_____

_____

_____

_____

_____

_____

_____

_____

GOD'S GREAT LOVE

Reflect

"GOD'S LOVE. AQUIFER FRESH. PURE AS APRIL SNOW.
ONE SWALLOW SLACKENS THE THIRSTY THROAT AND
SOFTENS THE CRUSTY HEART. IMMERSE A LIFE IN GOD'S
LOVE, AND WATCH IT EMERGE CLEANSED AND CHANGED.
WE KNOW THE IMPACT OF GOD'S LOVE. BUT THE
VOLUME? NO PERSON HAS EVER MEASURED IT."

What does it mean to immerse yourself in God's love? What does the
truth that God's love is measureless mean to you right now?

_____

_____

_____

_____

_____

_____

_____

_____

_____

Respond

When, if ever, did God's love become more than just a word to you?
When did it become deeply personal and real?

_____

_____

_____

_____

_____

_____

_____

_____

_____

_____

Pray and Praise

"But because of his great love for us, God, who is rich in mercy, made us alive with Christ even when we were dead in transgressions—it is by grace you have been saved."

(EPHESIANS 2:4-5)

_____

_____

_____

_____

_____

_____

_____

_____

_____

_____

_____

CHANGING YOUR LIFE
THROUGH LOVE

Reflect

"GOD KNOWS YOUR LIMITATIONS. HE'S WELL AWARE OF
YOUR WEAKNESSES. THAT'S WHY THE WORLD DOESN'T RELY
ON YOU. GOD LOVES YOU TOO MUCH TO SAY IT'S ALL
ABOUT YOU. . . . TO SAY 'IT'S NOT ABOUT YOU' IS NOT TO
SAY YOU AREN'T LOVED; QUITE THE CONTRARY. IT'S
BECAUSE GOD LOVES YOU THAT IT'S NOT ABOUT YOU."

How do you reconcile the two truths that we are special to God and
loved extravagantly by him, and yet "it's not about us"?

_____

_____

_____

_____

_____

_____

_____

_____

_____

Respond

How has experiencing God's great love in Christ prompted changes
in your life? In what way does the realization that life is not about you
free you up and reveal God's love for you?

_____

_____

_____

_____

_____

_____

_____

_____

_____

Pray and Praise

"This is how we know what love is: Jesus Christ laid down his life for us. And we ought to lay down our lives for our brothers. If anyone has material possessions and sees his brother in need but has no pity on him, how can the love of God be in him? Dear children, let us not love with words or tongue but with actions and in truth."

(1 JOHN 3:16–18)

_____

_____

_____

_____

_____

_____

_____

_____

_____

GOD'S MIRRORS

Reflect

"WE ARE [GOD'S] MIRRORS. TOOLS OF HEAVEN'S HELI-
OGRAPHY. REDUCE THE HUMAN JOB DESCRIPTION DOWN
TO ONE PHRASE AND THIS IS IT: REFLECT GOD'S GLORY."

The Bible says that we can *behold* God as in a mirror and we can *reflect* his glory like a mirror. The former phrase conveys the idea of contemplating God's glory, while the latter idea emphasizes our need to refract God's glory. What does the analogy of being a mirror of God's glory mean to you?

_____

_____

_____

_____

_____

_____

_____

_____

_____

_____

Respond

Think about your daily schedule. In everyday life, what are some
ways you can reflect God's glory and brightness?

_____

_____

_____

_____

_____

_____

_____

_____

_____

_____

Pray and Praise

"And all of us have had that veil removed so that we can be mirrors that brightly reflect the glory of the Lord. And as the Spirit of the Lord works within us, we become more and more like him and reflect his glory even more."

(2 CORINTHIANS 3:18 NLT)

_____

_____

_____

_____

_____

_____

_____

_____

_____

_____

_____

_____

LETTING YOUR LIGHT SHINE

Reflect

"UPON BEHOLDING GOD, MOSES COULD NOT HELP BUT
REFLECT GOD. *THE BRIGHTNESS HE SAW WAS THE BRIGHTNESS HE
BECAME.* BEHOLDING LED TO BECOMING. BECOMING LED TO
REFLECTING. . . . BEHOLDING GOD'S GLORY, THEN, IS NO
SIDE LOOK OR OCCASIONAL GLANCE; THIS BEHOLDING
IS A SERIOUS PONDERING."

Moses' life shone bright for God because he beheld God's glory. How
does "beholding" lead to "becoming"? Why does it matter that we pay
attention to what and who we spend time with?

_____

_____

_____

_____

_____

_____

_____

_____

_____

Respond

Jesus encouraged his followers to "let your light shine before men, that they may see your good deeds and praise your Father in heaven" (Matthew 5:16). Think about your life over the last week—your actions, your words, your encounters with others. In what ways are you shining and reflecting his love? How have you pointed people to God?

_____

_____

_____

_____

_____

_____

_____

_____

Pray and Praise

"Do everything without complaining or arguing,
so that you may become blameless and pure,
children of God without fault in a crooked and
depraved generation, in which you shine like stars
in the universe as you hold out the word of life."

(PHILIPPIANS 2:14–16)

_____

_____

_____

_____

_____

_____

_____

_____

_____

_____

_____

_____

MY MESSAGE IS ABOUT HIM

Reflect

"NOTHING MATTERED MORE TO PAUL THAN THE GOSPEL.
PAUL EXISTED TO DELIVER THE MESSAGE. HOW PEOPLE
REMEMBERED HIM WAS SECONDARY. . . . HOW PEOPLE
REMEMBERED CHRIST WAS PRIMARY. PAUL'S MESSAGE
WAS NOT ABOUT HIMSELF. HIS MESSAGE WAS
ALL ABOUT CHRIST."

What message is your life all about? What do you think enabled the apostle Paul to lift up Christ and not himself?

_____

_____

_____

_____

_____

_____

_____

_____

_____

Respond

When you're out with friends or at a social function, what is the primary impression you are seeking to make? How can you spread the message about Christ?

_____

_____

_____

_____

_____

_____

_____

_____

_____

_____

Pray and Praise

"But thanks be to God, who always leads us in
triumphal procession in Christ and through us
spreads everywhere the fragrance of the knowledge
of him. For we are to God the aroma of Christ
among those who are being saved and
those who are perishing."

(2 CORINTHIANS 2:14−15)

_____

_____

_____

_____

_____

_____

_____

_____

_____

_____

KNOWING YOUR LIFE MESSAGE

Reflect

"'WHAT ARE PEOPLE THINKING OF YOU?' A DEADLY QUERY.
WHAT THEY THINK OF YOU MATTERS NOT. WHAT THEY
THINK OF GOD MATTERS ALL. GOD WILL NOT SHARE HIS
GLORY WITH ANOTHER (ISAIAH 42:8). . . . GOD DOESN'T
NEED YOU AND ME TO DO HIS WORK. WE ARE EXPEDIENT
MESSENGERS, AMBASSADORS BY HIS KINDNESS, NOT BY OUR
CLEVERNESS. NEXT TIME YOU NEED A NUDGE AWAY FROM
THE SPOTLIGHT, REMEMBER: *YOU ARE SIMPLY ONE LINK
IN A CHAIN, AN UNIMPORTANT LINK AT THAT.*"

How does it make you feel that God doesn't need us, and that we are
simply messengers of God's good news? How do you distinguish between what people think of you and what they think of Christ?

_____

_____

_____

_____

_____

_____

_____

_____

Respond

How much do you worry about what people think of you? What
steps can you take to make your life message all about God and not
about you?

_____

_____

_____

_____

_____

_____

_____

_____

_____

Pray and Praise

"So the one who plants is not important, and the one who waters is not important. Only God, who makes things grow, is important."

(1 CORINTHIANS 3 : 7 NCV)

_____

_____

_____

_____

_____

_____

_____

_____

_____

_____

_____

MY SALVATION IS ABOUT HIM

Reflect

"CAN YOU ADD ANYTHING TO THIS SALVATION? NO. THE
WORK IS FINISHED. CAN YOU EARN THIS SALVATION? NO.
DON'T DISHONOR GOD BY TRYING. DARE WE BOAST
ABOUT THIS SALVATION? BY NO MEANS. THE GIVER OF
BREAD, NOT THE BEGGAR, DESERVES PRAISE. 'LET HIM WHO
BOASTS BOAST IN THE LORD' (1 CORINTHIANS 1:31). IT'S
NOT ABOUT WHAT WE DO; IT'S ALL ABOUT WHAT HE DOES."

How does it dishonor God by trying to earn our salvation? Why is it
crucial that you trust *only* in Christ?

_____

_____

_____

_____

_____

_____

_____

_____

_____

Respond

What things or people do you find yourself trusting in besides Christ
for your salvation? How might things change if you really understood
that your salvation is all about Christ and not what you have done?

_____

_____

_____

_____

_____

_____

_____

_____

_____

_____

Pray and Praise

"When we were utterly helpless, Christ came at just the right time and died for us sinners. . . . So now we can rejoice in our wonderful new relationship with God—all because of what our Lord Jesus Christ has done for us in making us friends of God."

(ROMANS 5:6, 11 NLT)

FACING YOUR BATTLE
WITH SELFISHNESS

Reflect

"LEGALISM. THE THEOLOGY OF 'JESUS +.' LEGALISTS
DON'T DISMISS CHRIST. THEY TRUST IN CHRIST A LOT.
BUT THEY DON'T TRUST IN CHRIST ALONE. LEGALISM IS
JOYLESS BECAUSE LEGALISM IS ENDLESS. . . . INMATES
INCARCERATED IN SELF-SALVATION FIND WORK BUT
NEVER JOY. . . . GRACE, HOWEVER, DISPENSES PEACE.
THE CHRISTIAN TRUSTS A FINISHED WORK. YOUR
SALVATION SHOWCASES GOD'S MERCY. IT MAKES
NOTHING OF YOUR EFFORT BUT EVERYTHING OF HIS."

Legalism is the prideful tendency and need to contribute something
to our own salvation. How are your own efforts at odds with God's
mercy? What does it mean to "showcase" God's mercy and grace?

_____

_____

_____

_____

_____

_____

_____

Respond

How is God helping you win the battle against your selfish pride and accept his grace? What are some ways you more actively reflect God's grace and mercy to others in your life?

_____

_____

_____

_____

_____

_____

_____

_____

_____

Pray and Praise

"God saved you by his special favor when you believed. And you can't take credit for this; it is a gift from God. Salvation is not a reward for the good things we have done, so none of us can boast about it."

(EPHESIANS 2:8–9 NLT)

_____

_____

_____

_____

_____

_____

_____

_____

_____

_____

DAY 22
MY BODY IS ABOUT HIM

Reflect

"WHEN IT COMES TO OUR BODIES, THE BIBLE
DECLARES THAT WE DON'T OWN THEM. . . . USE YOUR
BODY TO INDULGE YOUR PASSIONS? GRAB ATTENTION?
EXPRESS YOUR OPINIONS? NO. USE YOUR BODY TO HONOR
GOD. . . . YOUR BODY IS GOD'S INSTRUMENT, INTENDED
FOR HIS WORK AND FOR HIS GLORY."

How do you respond to the biblical teaching that God owns your
body, not you? How do the physical (body) and spiritual (soul) affect
each other?

_____

_____

_____

_____

_____

_____

_____

_____

_____

Respond

If your body is all about God and for his glory, do the activities and
choices in your life reflect that truth? Are any changes needed?

_____

_____

_____

_____

_____

_____

_____

_____

_____

_____

_____

Pray and Praise

"You surely know that your body is a temple where the Holy Spirit lives. The Spirit is in you and is a gift from God. You are no longer your own. God paid a great price for you. So use your body to honor God."

(1 CORINTHIANS 6:19–20 CEV)

_____

_____

_____

_____

_____

_____

_____

_____

_____

_____

MAKING YOUR BODY A HOLY PLACE

Reflect

"MAINTAIN GOD'S INSTRUMENT. FEED IT. REST IT. WHEN
HE NEEDS A STURDY IMPLEMENT——A SERVANT WHO IS
RESTED ENOUGH TO SERVE, FUELED ENOUGH TO WORK,
ALERT ENOUGH TO THINK——LET HIM FIND ONE IN YOU."

What does it mean to you that your body is God's holy instrument?
Why is it important to take care of our bodies?

_____

_____

_____

_____

_____

_____

_____

_____

_____

_____

Respond

What sort of instrument are you? How are you currently resting and refueling your body?

_____

_____

_____

_____

_____

_____

_____

_____

_____

Pray and Praise

"If you keep yourself pure, you will be a utensil God can use for his purpose. Your life will be clean, and you will be ready for the Master to use you for every good work."

(2 TIMOTHY 2:21 NLT)

_____

_____

_____

_____

_____

_____

_____

_____

_____

_____

_____

MY STRUGGLES ARE ABOUT HIM

Reflect

"THE BLIND MAN TO WHOM JESUS GAVE SIGHT WAS THE FRAME IN WHICH JESUS' POWER WAS SEEN, THE STAND UPON WHICH JESUS' MIRACLE WAS PLACED. BORN SIGHTLESS TO DISPLAY HEAVEN'S STRENGTH. . . . YOUR PAIN [ALSO] HAS A PURPOSE. YOUR PROBLEMS, STRUGGLES, HEARTACHES, AND HASSLES COOPERATE TOWARD ONE END—THE GLORY OF GOD."

How do you respond to the idea that God has a purpose even in pain and suffering?

_____

_____

_____

_____

_____

_____

_____

_____

_____

Respond

What's more common in your life—pursuing relief from life's problems, or pursuing God in the midst of problems and promoting his righteous reputation no matter what?

_____

_____

_____

_____

_____

_____

_____

_____

_____

Pray and Praise

"In your struggle against sin, you have not yet resisted to the point of shedding your blood. And you have forgotten that word of encouragement that addresses you as sons: 'My son, do not make light of the Lord's discipline, and do not lose heart when he rebukes you, because the Lord disciplines those he loves, and he punishes everyone he accepts as a son.' Endure hardship as discipline; God is treating you as sons."

(H E B R E W S   1 2 : 4 – 7)

_____

_____

_____

_____

_____

_____

_____

_____

USING YOUR SUFFERING FOR GLORY

Reflect

"A SEASON OF SUFFERING IS A SMALL ASSIGNMENT WHEN
COMPARED TO THE REWARD. RATHER THAN BEGRUDGE
YOUR PROBLEM, EXPLORE IT. PONDER IT. AND MOST OF
ALL, USE IT. USE IT TO THE GLORY OF GOD."

How can exploring and pondering a problem change your perspective on it? How does one use suffering to glorify God?

_____

_____

_____

_____

_____

_____

_____

_____

_____

_____

Respond

What kind of suffering are you going through today? What does it mean in your situation to use your problem for God's glory?

_____

_____

_____

_____

_____

_____

_____

_____

_____

_____

Pray and Praise

"Because of the LORD's great love we are
not consumed, for his compassions never fail.
They are new every morning; great is your faithfulness. . . . It is good for a man to bear the yoke
while he is young. Let him sit alone in silence,
for the LORD has laid it on him. . . . Though
he brings grief, he will show compassion,
so great is his unfailing love."

(LAMENTATIONS 3:22—23,
27—28, 32)

_____

_____

_____

_____

_____

_____

_____

_____

MY SUCCESS IS ABOUT HIM

Reflect

"FROM WHERE DOES SUCCESS COME? GOD. 'IT IS THE
LORD YOUR GOD WHO GIVES YOU POWER TO BECOME
RICH.' AND WHY DOES HE GIVE IT? FOR HIS REPUTATION.
'TO FULFILL THE COVENANT HE MADE WITH YOUR ANCES-
TORS.' GOD BLESSED ISRAEL IN ORDER TO BILLBOARD HIS
FAITHFULNESS. . . . THEIR SUCCESS ADVERTISED GOD.
NOTHING HAS CHANGED. GOD LETS YOU EXCEL
SO YOU CAN MAKE HIM KNOWN."

What is your measure or criteria for true success? What do you think
God's criteria for real success is?

_____

_____

_____

_____

_____

_____

_____

_____

Respond

In what ways has God blessed you with success? How can you use your successes more effectively to "billboard his faithfulness"?

_____

_____

_____

_____

_____

_____

_____

_____

_____

_____

_____

Pray and Praise

"Riches and honor come from you alone, for you rule over everything. Power and might are in your hand, and it is at your discretion that people are made great and given strength."

(1 CHRONICLES 29:12 NLT)

_____

_____

_____

_____

_____

_____

_____

_____

_____

_____

_____

REDEFINING YOUR IDEA OF SUCCESS

Reflect

"WHY ARE YOU GOOD AT WHAT YOU DO? FOR YOUR COM-
FORT? FOR YOUR RETIREMENT? FOR YOUR SELF-ESTEEM?
NO. DEEM THESE AS BONUSES, NOT AS THE REASON. WHY
ARE YOU GOOD AT WHAT YOU DO? FOR GOD'S SAKE.
YOUR SUCCESS IS NOT ABOUT WHAT YOU DO. IT'S
ABOUT HIS PRESENT AND FUTURE GLORY."

Do you tend to see your achievements as your own doing, or the
result of your own intelligence and hard work? Why? Compare that
to the basis and purpose of success by biblical standards.

_____

_____

_____

_____

_____

_____

_____

_____

_____

Respond

How do you respond when you succeed; who gets the credit deep in
your heart? In what ways can you acknowledge more fully your bless-
ings as coming from God and thank him?

_____

_____

_____

_____

_____

_____

_____

_____

_____

_____

Pray and Praise

"Don't be deceived, my dear brothers. Every good and perfect gift is from above, coming down from the Father of the heavenly lights, who does not change like shifting shadows."

(JAMES 1:16—17)

_____

_____

_____

_____

_____

_____

_____

_____

_____

_____

UPWARD THINKING

Reflect

"THE AMBASSADOR HAS A SINGULAR AIM—TO REPRESENT HIS KING. HE PROMOTES THE KING'S AGENDA, PROTECTS THE KING'S REPUTATION, AND PRESENTS THE KING'S WILL. THE AMBASSADOR ELEVATES THE NAME OF THE KING. MAY WE HAVE NO HIGHER GOAL THAN TO SEE SOMEONE THINK MORE HIGHLY OF OUR FATHER, OUR KING."

Do you agree that there is no higher goal than to help others look upward and think more highly of God? Why or why not?

_____

_____

_____

_____

_____

_____

_____

_____

_____

_____

Respond

As a Christian ambassador, what does it mean in practical terms to promote your heavenly King's agenda, protect his reputation, and present his will?

_____

_____

_____

_____

_____

_____

_____

_____

_____

Pray and Praise

"I urge you to live a life worthy of the
calling you have received. Be completely humble
and gentle; be patient, bearing with one another
in love. Make every effort to keep the unity of
the Spirit through the bond of peace."

(EPHESIANS 4:1–3)

_____

_____

_____

_____

_____

_____

_____

_____

_____

_____

RETHINKING YOUR WAY TO HAPPINESS

Reflect

"SELF-PROMOTION. SELF-PRESERVATION.
SELF-CENTEREDNESS. . . . WE THOUGHT SELF-CELEBRATION
WOULD MAKE US HAPPY. . . . THE MOON MODELS OUR
ROLE. THE MOON REFLECTS THE GREATER LIGHT. AND
SHE'S HAPPY TO DO SO! MAY GOD RESCUE US FROM SELF-
CENTERED THINKING. AFTER ALL, IT'S NOT ABOUT . . .
WELL, YOU CAN FINISH THE SENTENCE."

Why does self-celebration not make us happy? What does it mean to
delight in reflecting Christ?

_____

_____

_____

_____

_____

_____

_____

_____

_____

Respond

How does living for God's glory help you rethink what it means to be truly happy and fulfilled?

_____

_____

_____

_____

_____

_____

_____

_____

_____

Pray and Praise

"Trust in the LORD and do good; dwell in the land and enjoy safe pasture. Delight yourself in the LORD and he will give you the desires of your heart. Commit your way to the LORD; trust in him and he will do this: He will make your righteousness shine like the dawn, the justice of your cause like the noonday sun."

(PSALM 37:3–6)

_____

_____

_____

_____

_____

_____

_____

_____

CONCLUSION

One last time: Life is *not* about us. It's all about God. Our days are not about our comfort or desires; they are about God's glory. What a joy and relief that truth is!

You have recorded ways God has challenged you to make his priorities your own. You have jotted down questions and insights and prayer requests. But you will miss out on some of the most important aspects of journaling if, along with this book, you shelf what you've learned and let it collect dust. James 1:23–25 says:

> "Anyone who listens to the word but does not do what it says is like a man who looks at his face in a mirror and, after looking at himself, goes away and immediately forgets what he looks like. But the man who looks intently into the perfect law that gives freedom, and continues to do this, not forgetting what he has heard, but doing it—he will be blessed in what he does."

Take time to periodically look back through these journal pages. Keep listening to God's Word and begin implementing what you've learned into your actions and choices and attitudes. Then you will know the real joy and freedom that comes when life is all about and for God.

As you end this journaling experience, what is one important truth or insight you are taking with you? What answered prayer have you realized?

_____

_____

_____

_____

_____

_____

_____

_____

_____

_____

_____

_____

_____